3/17/07

This cop[...]

who's who

vivid

is

for Shelli with an "I". I had an excellent time today and I hope you did as well. Here is my last blurt: magnolia!

— Matt

who's who

vivid

poems by matt hart

SLOPE EDITIONS
New Hampshire   New York   Massachusetts

Both the book's epigraph and the title of the poem "Giant Traumatism"
are by Guillaume Apollinaire, Shattuck, from SELECTED WRITINGS,
copyright © 1971 by Roger Shattuck. Reprinted by permission of New
Directions Publishing Corp.

Published by Slope Editions
www.slopeeditions.org

Library of Congress Cataloging-in-Publication Data

Hart, Matt, 1969-
  Who's who vivid : poems / by Matt Hart.
    p. cm.
  ISBN 0-9718219-9-2
  I. Title.

PS3608.A7864W48 2005
811'.6--dc22

                                    2005026598

Book design by Eric Appleby of HubcapArt.com
Cover photos by Chris LaCoe

Printed in the United States of America

9 8 7 6 5 4 3 2 1

FIRST EDITION

CONTENTS

I know nothing anymore and I can only love.

— Apollinaire

COMPLETELY BY ACCIDENT

I was in a fix.

I was sloshing with joy.

I was looking at my feet and my feet looked good.

I said to my apartment, "I am a tiger. I am an iron,"
then cleared my throat and hollered, "Yahtzee!"
into the jungle.

No vapors intervened to banish the quiet from my soul,
and nobody looked in the mailbox either.

I have always understood "nothing" as a series of zeroes

and imagine the clouds as if I myself were a cloud,
as the hiss of a slow-leaking tire requires.

No one delivers the ice that I ordered.
No one controls my remote from the forest.

Where is my pet rock when I'm needing her the most?

My little retriever with a stone in her bladder?

From the myths of beginnings to possible worlds,
I have often been wrong about philosophy in public.

When I boiled this evening's lobster this morning,

I screamed and invented a monster.

IN THE GLOAMING

I was standing I was standing up.

I was picking my way through a puddle of *awk!*

I was well aware of the uneaten green beans
and they were well aware of my well-meaning intentions.

My mission: To save the most, the best-dressed for dessert,
to assert myself in the gloaming, while wondering about gloaming
and looking it up and feeling all the while tangential.

I can barely see in this light
the new puppy named Daisy.

I'm not much in the way of understanding
the things I do or why that loaf of bread and not
this one with the sunflower seeds overwhelming.

Slip me the truth in a worn out roller coaster.

Give me a sound I can make with one cricket.

I've come to fix the sink. I've been freaking over a flower.

I thought my head was half its age.

The tide washes in/washes out.

THE WEIGHT OF MY NEXT BEST THING

Who weighs more: me or this twitching carp?
you or the buried beneath us? The way I see it,

something's gotta come to the surface, or one of us
gets a window smashed. I may be thirty-ish and still
interested in seashells, but not enough

to get sucked down the drain looking
for a rowboat with my head in the sand.

Nevertheless, if you get tired of your couch,
you can always come over and crash on mine.

Just don't expect any light-hearted chatter.
I can be an elephant when I need to be. I can spit

and deify. I mean, c'mon, I already say I love you
a thousand times a minute, and in spite of this
you still lack the proper definition. Obviously

there's a glitch in my lip. Both the ends
and the means are entirely unclear.

I swerve to miss the bolting deer,
and then can't remember your name.

(See previous final version: An ambulance drifts
up the driveway, and I follow it into the light.)

POEM WHERE THE MESSAGE TRAILS OFF

Once upon a time I was missing completely
and that time, once upon, was now.

In my shoes an intruder.
In my face a world of trees.

Whosoever may know these seas, row your boat out
to the meadow to meet me.

Do it soon, and do it quickly.
Don't stop to read this, please!

But how can I describe to you
the place where you can find me—

swimming in a birdbath,
burning out in my pajamas . . .

My love, I am calling long distance from a coma.
Does anybody out there have their ears on?

HOW I KNOW I'M STILL MISSING

Sometimes the gladiolas backfire in my face.

I get headaches for days when I read in the dark.

When I cross the bridge at midnight
I pretend I'm a sparrow escaping a star.

Escape is not something I ever take lightly.

Behind me is a light with a lampshade most grave.

I lay my eggs neatly in the crest of a wave
and tell them to wait there until I get home.
Sometimes they listen, sometimes they don't.

I open a door and pass through an elephant,
my hair full of dust and the shadows of bells.

Someone points out a large hole in my pocket.

On the teeter-totter I feel like a million bucks.

CRISS-CROSS IN EVERY DIRECTION

Miles all night in pigskin galoshes
we blemish, reiterate, reiterate.
It's simple, but it doesn't feel so good.

Or flanked on all sides by ambulance races,
sternums choke engines, but nobody's breathing—
not a goddamned word. Now the flat tire. Now

the out-of-focus dictionary. That's when
they intubate. That's when they dredge up
the black and white rainbows, the dead televisions.

I be addled and varied of red pen flowers.
I be mountains of oozing dread anthills. I fills
the boat with fire extinguishers and tries not to

trip over your yawns. One way to move a reader
is to smash a bottle across the bridge
of her nose. Another is through the careful use

of methodical, un-dramatized language.
Ultimately, rationality will convince her:
someday whales will beach on the moon.

Tomorrow I'll see "moon" misspelled on her eyelids.
Of course, I'm not holding my breath.

WHY I'M NOT A ROBOT

I rot. The poached elephant beside me rots.
His tusks have vanished,
but nobody knows where.
And just when the new dentistry
was coming into style!
Just when the cartoons
were exploding with noses! I smile
as I notice my guard coming down,
the wabbit peeking out of its wascally hole.
Sad as it may seem, I think I'm nearing the finish
where "Sad as it may seem" isn't really sad at all,
but rather, a triumph, a walk upon water.
Splendiferous owls who's who-ing on a rooftop.
The Ferris Wheel breaking my heart with its drone.

SELF-HELPER

When you've recovered
from your awkward silence
draw a circle and stick
your nose in the center
of the universe. Sniff around
the hem of its garment. Is it toxic?
Is it sincere? Record your answers
in the spaces provided. Now imagine
yourself in a garage surrounded by cats
and buckets of paint, lavender
and periwinkle and sea-sludge green.
Don't touch a thing. Are you in pain?
Take a huff of fixatif. Do you remember
the first person who broke your heart?
Well, s/he's back, and like always making tea
in your closet, singing cross-sections of birds,
cutting the tag off your mattress. Meanwhile you're up on the roof playing
language-games with your lips, asking directions
from the migrating ducks, combining the names
of streets and pets until finally you get
to Walnut Mescalito. With multiple illusions
reconfigure your libido: Gerbera daisies,
a brand new soul, the cosmos sucking
your esophagus whole. Then a ticker-tape
fortune pours out of a puppy.
There are no incorrect answers.

REVOLUTIONS PER MINUTE

Now, with dust in my hair, collecting marbles,
I see with renewed interest the devastating past
and the erasable future. O dust pan, O floor mop!
Cat toy. Ted Berrigan. Floating casino. I may
putter my life away, but at least these genuine antics
are genuine antics: antlers, wall sockets,
a wire brush tail— Who do I think I am?
My pockets full of violets never grow violent,
but always they grow by accident, like spots around
the edges of sunrise. I'm sick unto death
of keeping quiet in a jar. By now I should be
glowing and powdering my noses. By now
every one of us should be totally ajar.
O Hamlet! O Juliet! Wherefore art thou,
removable Spot? The blur I feel in the face
of all our greatest tragedies is merely the punchline to a beautiful joke: paintcan, sour apple, Zurich.
Tristan Tzara Tristan Tzara Tristan Tzara. Welcome
to America, may I take your order. I don't want to
destroy anything, not even a paperclip. My incredible,
stylish pajamas keep me warm in the night,
and joy is the antidote to everything else.
I laugh, I sing it, my monster-big mouth!
In the face of the face of the new-fangled machinery
my Star-Spangled Fruit Loops wear everybody out.
I'll substitute your everything for my colossal nothing.
I'll make my revolutions your problem.

ELEPHANT

That the elephant's upon me is no accident.
I've been wishing this big game on myself
for a long time, reinforcing the floors,
marking clearly the exits. So come on out,
Loxodonta africana/Elephas maximus,
I know you're in here. What is it you want
to talk about? Ponderous participles, clumsy
quotations? I've been putting you off for weeks,
but now you're too much? Let the games begin.
I've already told you I'm terrible at anything
that involves strategic thinking. But did you know
that in the Chinese version of chess there's a game-piece
modeled on you? I can't remember whether
it's the knight or the rook, but sometimes it runs amok
across the board trampling everyone, including
the royal family and the human cannonball.
Anyway, I'm sorry. You'd be better off playing
the poachers. At least they engage the text and con-
jugate correctly. If you want to find them
they're over in that white space just off to the left.
Today they're disguised as crows, tomorrow
gazelles or *delirium tremens.* People say elephants
never forget— is this true? I don't forget much either,
and I believe everything I hear, to boot. But with you
is remembering always knowing how to walk tail-in-trunk
with your fellows in a circle, or do specific instances
pop uncontrollably into your head, like having giant
ears as a kid and being called Dumbo, or
the night your mother sacrificed herself
so that you could escape from the fire? Hey, Elephant,
are you still with me? You might as well keep
staying at my place. At least here you're safe
from predators, and no poacher, even out of his mind,
would expect to find you living in a row house
in inner city Ohio. You like it here don't you?
With your view of the skyline. With your tusks
in their place. Elephant, my little secret, you aren't
even pink. Thank you for coming to my party.

BEAUTIFUL BURNS

To discover again my fragile mind, the one
in red floodlights and Paul Valery's top hat,

I'll have to stop swimming in the sink of
the couch of the . . . scratch that. See the way

she twirls her headdress like a heliotropic owl?
What's beautiful burns a hole in my pocket,

my esophagus, my icebox only slightly.
It's late Saturday night after too much TV.

My vocabulary suffers big time. Nowadays
in everything the emphasis is on hipsterish

tragedy, but it's all so fake my head hurts.
I know everybody, but nobody knows me.

It's sunshine or it's snowing, and "it's" is a place-
holder for the ugly barometer. Preoccupied ever

I drip peppermint ice cream on my shoelaces,
as the birds' nests beneath me crackle with soul

and dirigibles vanish from the next day's parties.
Most of this I got from a song I never liked much,

something oh baby with a fork in you dearly.
The scarecrow's rain boots are ridiculous/delicious,

like fathoming sadness from nothing in particular
just to make something that stutters sincerely.

WISHERLY

My soul is in my cervix...
But even as I say it I realize it can never be.
Not to mention that my eggs are in the cake batter
and that I beat them beforehand in a kind of reverse
creation, making the end a beginning
and the beginning an end. All I know is that
yesterday I could barely see my pelvis
in front of my safety goggles, and now I can
see perfectly that it's covered with white frosting
and fairy dust. Idling lung. Collapsible truck.
The body with age loses some of its elasticity,
some of its inner rooster. No more robot zapping a virus,
but instead a progenitor of inexplicable nuance.
Everybody and the world going haywire.
The sun comes up to fuck things up,
but apparently I'm the only one who thinks so.
My skeleton covered in screwballs. The nerve center
battered by cowlicks. Since when did I turn
into a snowman, the 20-something party
being out of the question? This fuselage of rocket ship
would've tasted better with lemon and a side
of medieval crisis. Ooh-ooh-ooh, cuckoo-ka-choo,
it is written. The best machines have multiple chambers
wherein chemical reactions make them worth more
than the sum of their parts. For instance,
tear ducts. Chicken hearts. Sometimes
they have special switches which allow them to move
exactly backwards. World War I. Ancient Rome.
Terrible lizard. Maybe a little dancing
in the twilight's last glimmer. Thou shalt not
fertilize. Let there be cake.

SHAG CARPET GALA

Hello, Mr. Smith. Hello, Mrs. Jones.
We've got a thing going on.
I think I need my scissors.
The world in a swirl.
Ice cream on the wall.
Watch out for the banana peel on the escalator,
and watch out for the remains of the mouse behind
the refrigerator, too. I'm not trying to be bossy.
I don't believe in authority figures. They're like symbols,
and symbols I don't believe in either. As a result,
my best efforts at interpreting texts always fail,
because I can't let myself see beneath the waves.
I fall asleep on the surface before the depths
catch my breath. I couldn't care less
about crushed flowers or expired milk, and definitely not
about the importance allotted to images by artists.
But when you say eternity and then twirl your body,
forcing your dress to come up over your knees,
I feel immediately an expressive urge
to respond with singing, but singing
with all of my might in your ear.
To me it feels like hitting you with a hammer.
And what do you care, being almost deaf?
Can defeat be nearly as close as it feels?
What about the end? Is there anything left
to get worked up about in the world?
While you're thinking, I'll stare like death at the passing parade.
Oom-pah, darling, says the beautiful tuba,
killing two birds with one brain.

AS WITH EVERYTHING WE LOVE

Someone says sparrow blown against a wall.
Someone says comparison. Then we're staring
at a portrait of two acrobats
on a scarlet background with flowers. We put on
our shoes of the alarmed. Someone falls
and someone shatters. At dinner, we revel

in the taste of Chianti, and the men who drag
the depths of the sea overcome us.
I say your name like a charm, and you say
I'm reading too much into sorrow,
the flashlight beam and the basket of fruit.

Then someone punches a hole
in my best attempt at a counterexample.
We sob all evening over glitter on the floor.
I can't help confessing anymore

my aversion to sour candy, my allergy
to honey bees, my anxiety at the sight of a hard hat.
You bring up daddy long-leggers and two stones
with one bird, but only briefly. I follow
with ice-chewers and mud slides

in the night. Somehow we realize, almost
at the same time, without repeating ourselves,
we're going around in a circle. Without
repeating ourselves, we're playing to the crowd
that never gathers or applauds. Think of it
as a movie, you say, so blue sometimes it's white.

TWINGE

I remember we both had coffee
and talked a little while
about steam pointing back to a process.
Already the incident involving the traveling salesman
had ended abruptly in a smear of yogurt,
but Leda dripped on as a reminder that
discomfort and aesthetics often come disguised
as final arias, puffs of pastry, three deep breaths
in the shape of a rabbit. I forget who said it,
but I remember distinctly that one of us used
the word *clash* in two different contexts.
Much remains hidden: sharks, white blood cells,
and what you meant when you gestured
to the sky with your pelvis. The loops
indicate the moment of not getting into bed.
The blue to blot out the black. The black
to remember the wedding. The wedding
to forget how fleas must feel. From here I can still see
Prometheus spinning, but what he was wearing
is almost invisible, the afterglow of fashion, which means
flooding in a language I've forgotten. Maybe one of us
should've noted the time. At some point, I remember,
I got tired of holding water, and a collision ensued:
sad white dwarf with an Easy Bake oven.
Or was it a scarf with an egg-pink backdrop?
I forget. I remember that you offered me a chair
but it was folded in the shape of a centaur.
Adding all those zeros only made things worse.
The word *twinge* was employed in an act of desperation.
Why can't we remember the things we remember?

IN FIFTEEN MINUTES

I'll see your blue dress and raise you
by your hair into the clouds, where we'll eat
peppermints and fall apart for no reason.

It won't hurt, but dizziness may occur, cough
drops may fall, birds may think we're crazy.
But what do birds know? At best they sing

only one or two songs. They pass over so many
construction sites, blood clots, tidal waves—
they don't have any idea what we go through,

what we commit ourselves to; I'm pale with it.
Getting anywhere in fifteen minutes is impossible,
so I applaud you for forcing my face through

the window. Unfortunately, I'm stuck.
I can only see fire and the aforementioned clouds.
It seems everything these days is merely fire and clouds,

clouds and fire in a full length mirror. Today at work
there was so little for me to do, I swept the floor
four or five times. One woman said she could see herself in it.

Later somebody spilled some water and somebody else
slipped and fell and started leaking. That's when I ran
to get the baking soda and subsequently missed

the flower delivery. That's when I broke
through the overwhelmed ceiling
and did what I could to get you alone.

APOLOGY CRISIS

When I flipped on the power
the impression of a miraculous intervention
was an unfortunate and immediate side effect,
causing my defenses to crash and your resistance

to plummet. I'm sorry. What you experienced was merely
the silo door opening, the grain spilling out, the hatchling
taking its first ever breath. Tonight would've been
our celebration of the fluttering mixed signals.

I'd have worn my reticular tie, and you
your numerous powders. All the misery between
us would've dissolved in the strobe lights,
my breath on your furnace, your fork

in my socket. If only we had understood
the new system sooner. How under the new system
there's a new system. And how under the newer system,

a flock of geese comes between us, then a mobile home,
a tomahawk... both of us ashamed in the morning.

WHO'S WHO VIVID IN THE MOONLIGHT
IN PAIN

Who's who vivid in the moonlight in pain—
too late I uncovered the nothing above me.
    Now jumping for joy in the muck overwhelming
    and singing inside me for all that I'm worth

        (and with death to keep me honest),
        I walketh the stairs with my brother King Kong
        as alphabet blocks spill out of my pocket
        and spell not much— no particular world.
        Hooray! Hooray!

        to discover at last: nothing's my fault,
        and what's more, there's nothing to help it
    get clean. Enamored, then enchanted, but in the morning
I'm a shoe lace. And in the afternoon, I'm the building's

        unbuilding, the butcher, a sweater of man
    in the bluing. Goddamn it, my darling, everyday
I come to you conflicted, and I'm sorry. I kiss you
on the fire escape, out into the yard. How

uncomfortable to be comfortable, to be churning
    with poems, to be messed-up and messy,
        exuberant-green... Anymore what I mean
        is like new, wet cement.
        I speak and I'm stuck in it forever.

DADA'S SAWED-OFF HALF BROTHER

Take any line. Cut it off.
Take any new line, set it
to music, set it ablaze.
Watch it collapse into settle and haze
and forget about vision. Instead be prepared
to appear as applesauce. Be prepared
to tell us why you waltz. Cut it off at the
Boy Scout motto. Add the phrase,
To turn red, as in hot communista,
as in delicious suspect, as in
laundromat heaven. Cut off everything
before the word laundromat and everything
after the la of laundromat. Now sing
La Fortunato in the gutter. Now sing
Why are all the radicals crying?
Answer: Because they've lost their
shells of chocolate cool, their
yard-long tongues of provocative dust.
Make a line, if you will, a cut
in the dust. Let go of everything
but the whistle. Make it
wistful, make somebody sigh.
Make a mask out of oranges
and scare with it. Make cry.
Use extreme caution with amputation.
Cut up and modified, one gets amplified
and putative. One begins to break. Generous
association reveals, A needle exists.
Amplify the needle, then cut it
to pieces. Am punctured, living fury.
Therefore, need lemons. My heart won't
stop crowing at the crack of dawn.
My voice won't stop cracking at the sight
of blood. O beautiful for spacious. Cut off.

BREAKABLE SWAN

The next thing I notice is the swan in three pieces.
Three black and white triangles
and a face in the mist of a misspelled word.
(Of course I soon get bored with this.)

It's been a month since last I was relentless
in my armored eyelids and club-like tail.
Now I drink something lukewarm
out of a cup the color of trailer park.

How funny it feels to drift off dark and go dripping.
I stop and scoop up magic beans. I screw
and unscrew silver lids. In the distance a foghorn,
and all the while I'm tracing shapes

in the air with a dessert fork. Triangle, Triangle
let down your hair! But she never does. When I look
I see strangers, soft light and nectarines. Sometimes
I see artificial snowballs and broken sea men.

Sometimes I'm a useful mistake. Sometimes... May I
cut in? I'm looking for the town just over
that seashell, the cottony death called pink inside.
Back outside, I spread salt on the stairs. Half-automatically

they're stars. I'm trying to sell me what I already have.
I can't see my hands for the breakable swan.

LETTER TO A FRIEND WHO I'LL NEVER
SEE AGAIN

I keep scanning the sky for a glimpse of you spinning,
but after a few minutes when you don't appear
I go back to what Breton said about the magnificence
of waiting, and about the love of the irrational

and the irrational of love. From there, Wittgenstein's preface
in the *Philosophical Investigations* is a cake walk,
especially the part about going, "criss-cross in every direction
over a wide field of thought." With that in mind

I do hope you'll forgive me for ripping off your Paris poem.
Though this isn't a poem, it's a letter; I'm insisting.
No copies will be made. I will not send it out. But if I do
I will send it to you, where it can be appreciated

or ridiculed the most. How strange it is trying on
someone else's voice, and yet stranger that it's easier
than wearing one's own. I have only three pairs of shoes,
which is laughable, I know. And one of those is missing

its laces. I bet you have lots of shoes and all manner
of dresses, ones that anyone would be lucky to see.
In New York City, where you live, there are many sites
worth noting, your dresses (I'm sure) being only one of them.

There's also the Statue of Liberty, The Met, and KGB
— if you're into that sort of thing. I haven't been
to New York in years, though the last time I was there,
my friend Flaviano punched a hole in a wall. But the story

of how that came to happen isn't nearly as interesting as the fact
that he punched a hole in the wall in a hole in the wall.
It was in the East Village at a club called Tony's or Strawberry
Pie Filling or something equally obvious and obnoxious.

Our band had just played, and the owner wouldn't pay us.
A month later, the place was closed. I like to think
it leaked to death, which probably isn't far from the truth,
as the owner was an intravenous drug user. Those guys

never win, but often they don't pay the bands that play
in their clubs either. It seems that hard drug use
doesn't preclude liking music, but it does dictate
what one does with one's money. I don't have any

money, but if I did, I would send you something other
than bootlegs and manuscripts. I'm not sure what—
maybe flowers, but in a week they'd be dead, and what kind
of a gift is that? I can't think of anything worse

than giving flowers, as always they point to garbage
and the end, which are things I try hard not to think about.
Patti Smith called Gregory Corso a flower when he died,
which sounds lovely at first and then descends quickly

into nonsense and loss. Corso, whose poetry nobody cares about
but me, said that, "Spontaneity in poetry is notes, not poems."
And I'm sure he'd say the same about gift-giving, letter writing, etc.
Like everything else, this started out with fire, but now I'm losing

steam. I'm tired of making the world up out of nothing. You said,
"Tell me what you believe in," in response to one of my poems.
I believe in nothing, and at the same time I believe that it's crucial
to believe in something in the face of nothing, and to live

with the consequences of that belief. Still, it's hard.
Even understanding that sentence is hard. I believe
in making indefensible statements and defending them
anyway. I believe in walking the blood red carpet. I believe

that art is about continuity and rupture and joy, and that
as James Longenbach says, "...poetry's greatest power
is to instill in us a craving for something other than poetry."
"I am the maker and destroyer of worlds,"— that's Shiva,

via J. Robert Oppenheimer. I have a million quotations
in my head: "Ruin is formal," "The slightest loss of attention
leads to death," "O bomb I love you," "There is no such thing
as a break down," "Everything turns into writing," "And I am

lost with you,"... I believe in every one of them, though
they don't amount to much. I apologize for all of this,
the letter-as-poem itself, but also for the apology
itself, because no one likes when writers either.

apologize for that which they're about to write, or
apologize for that which they've already written, or
apologize for that which they're in the process of writing.
Also, nobody likes quatrains. And I would never use them

in person. But in this letter I have found them to be
a necessity. I believe in the almighty zero. I believe
in inclusion rather than exclusion. I voted
for the Democrats in the most recent election, even though

my own politics are much more left wing. As you know,
the trick to a letter like this is figuring a way to end it
that pushes the content forward, while simultaneously acting
as a summary of it. I cannot do this. I wouldn't know

where to start, and I'm far too impatient to think about it.
I'm not being clever, but rather just the opposite.
I'm telling you I love you, but it sounds like a rant.

It sounds like somebody plastered in Ohio.
This is how I've burned all my bridges.

I WAS DUMB WITH PEARLS, I WAS DUMB

I was dumb with pearls, I was dumb.
I was steaming mussels, or rather, ironing bathing suits
in a hurry. I was responsible for the fisherman's ball.
It was a sort of dance-stew. And they were crying
over you, as I was crying over the laundry without a coat on
in the surf. All night was spicy, a little sweet,

a little flooded. I was wearing my new socks
with the half-assed crabs embroidered on the heels.
I was ridiculously attending a conference.

All the morning after, you resisted my advances.
Elegant red chair in the corner on drugs.
Lamp like it was wilting. Speed, I think, kills, you said,
as another nervous doe popped out between your legs.
An adjustable rake. A new toaster oven. All
were run over in a matter of seconds, while I was

baking cakes for comedians who were themselves
half-baked, telling jokes about starlets
to a swimming pool of sea men. I was fishing

for announcements, ripe nuts and sweet berries.
I moved to the middle of the subdivision, and there
I subdivided, became three goats in one. What was
funny stayed funny, because nothing was funny
anymore. I was your man, and we were awfully sad.
I was boiling peanuts and bluebirds for the big game

on Sunday. I was a mess of bright lights and redecorated
walls. Physical prowess had never been one of my
strengths, and now it would have to wait until spring

everlasting. I was famished. I was taking the enemy
blue cheese in a bag, wanting a friend more than anything else.
In one of my stanzas, which is now lost, a rabbit jumped
over a kernel of truth. Before that I had no contact
with philosophers whatsoever. None of my stories
had satisfactory endings, the punch in the bowl, the punch

in my nose. Punch filled a gap by connecting a line
with blood— I was saying marine, and then it turned out
I wasn't available for comment. I was a tugboat

singing in strain. O gasoline are you listening? I was drifting
in and out of a time card for years. What, in fact,
was my reason for living? I often asked myself to hold it down.
I was saying something bashful, I was saying something coy.
I was looking for clams in the hem of your dress.
I was swallowing oysters with lemon on the moon.

Everything I ignored turned out to be central.
I was occupying Asia at a terrifying rate. I was
terrifically overblown! I was giddy

with an ulcer. Not much of a geezer,
from the start I was finished.

GREAT WHITE SHARK

For I will consider you, great white shark.
For you are the best engineered for your business.
For in warm seas there is no mouth more primary, nor teeth
    more inclusive.
For you bite off the bloom in the straggler's pocket, the trail of
    blood, the watch that won't quit.
For the wounded attract you as a consolation prize.
For you begin life rather bluely and whiten with age.
For your smile is the great part.
For your love is the shock love of pieces adrift, pieces of sunset,
    pieces of spleen.
For you never make an unfair distinction at meal time.
For having no use for manners, you chew boldly with your
    mouth open, and having evolved over time into a true
    aesthete, digest the artery along with the art.
For in fact you were among the first to appreciate Van Gogh,
    calling his ear a matter of taste.
For the ocean is your swimming pool, and we are poor suckers.
For scientifically speaking you are the holiest mackerel,
    Carcharodon carcharias of the class *Chondrichthyes.*
For holy is the mackerel the size of a truck.
For following your mouth is your monument tail.
For in the dictionary, depending on where one looks, you sit
    between great uncle and great year, or alternately,
    between white sea bass and white slave.
For you are five words removed from white space and seven from
    white potato.
For in the same breath you are the underworld's warning to heaven.
For Giant Shark is a term of the Devil Flounder.
For you are an instrument upon which the children can blame
    the missing.
For instance, consider a cat named Jeoffry Considering.
For better yet, a mouthful of Christopher Smart.
For indeed you are the quickest to your mark of any creature.
For you are ferocious to boiling, of gravity and swagger.
For first you serenade the swimmer or seal.
For second you size the heft of your jaws.
For third John Williams beats two notes to death, conducting
    wild bubbles in a race to the surface.
For fourth the others are too busy squealing.
For fifth you forget to say grace out of habit.

For sixth the music increases the torque.
For seventh you nudge the terrified monkey.
For eighth you consider your cavern of razors.
For ninth the end is a ripping to strings.
For tenth you say, What a wonderful meal.
For having considered and eaten it, the more must follow.
For it's all you can eat!
For the very next moment is overly famished.
For the bird of good omen is better with salt, as is the Ancient
      Mariner and the ghost of his ship, the floodgate of wine
      and the glinting of trinkets.
For your very own reflection is as much to be eaten again.
For your fusiform finish never stalls in high water.
For your machinery is constantly engaged with the crow's nest.
For your motions upon the face of the ocean are more gorgeous
      than any other predator's.
For the bleeding produced is always real.
For what escapes you drifts cleanly off the edge of the world.
For in your wake there is nothing left to mourn.
For your emotions are buoyant and your dance the craze.
For you do not hide.
For you do not creep.

NERVOUS ALUMINUM RABBIT

Does burn. Is burn. Ha! I stole that
from a friend, but I don't think she'll mind.
My mind, I'm convinced, is a shotgun:
prone to do damage at all the wrong times,
and accurate up to forty-five yards. Dear Melanie,
Hello. It's October, and I'm lost.
Nobody's singing well enough your birthday
to suit me. Let me correct that in my truly
incoherence [sic] voice: Dear Hart,
Good riddance. You're a robot with fangs.
It's 4:15 AM, and I've been up all night
talking talking talking like a parrot in its cage.
Is it true I should know better? Go ahead and feed the meter,
and when I get there we'll have snow peas for dinner.
Greetings Ridiculous, It's already November,
and somehow the crickets haven't frozen to death.
For hours they've been chirping and kicking up dust.
Earlier, I saw a fire truck going top speed across the lawn
with ambulances and cops in a line close behind.
It all made me a little tired, so I stopped
what I was doing— I was slanted, I was rhyming—
and laid down on the couch. How sensible.
And on an unrelated note, Dear Dog, Settle down.
Read a book, get drunk, bite the burs
in your fur. It occurs to me suddenly,
I am nearly in my winter, in deep hibernation
in a cloister of snow. Dear God/ Dear Damage,
The way you do me is uncertain, is enormous and painful.
Dear Snowball, Caterwauling, Deep-lake-zoo,
I am but a nervous, aluminum rabbit. Why
can't my mother understand this? Why is my father
asleep in his hole? O Dearly, I love you
no matter what I wrote in the note, no matter what
the slick attorney may say to the contrary. Dear Dead,
Hello. It feels good to be finished. Like a flower
with a head wound, I barely function when you're missing.
I start fires and then can't put them out by myself.

INC.

Strolling among wounded merchants' daughters.
What to buy? What to wear? The questions
dreadless enough, I take them down from their posts.
Heart cuff, woodpecker wing, suit-so-sorry.

News of the repeating, damned repeating,
circles the sky.
Once I tried crooning and fell apart simply.
The girls in slit skirts made an art of revealing.

In a world of sad weekends I'm the last flamingo
standing. My leg hurts. The weight of it.
If I have any memory at all, it's connected by slingshot
to piles of torn paper, the world in tails.

Scrape my dossier together for a sense of what sells.
Begin again with sulfur, dust-bunnies in bloom.
I wait in my room for myself to return.
Outside in the rain she is grinning.

BIG DEATH

I've put the daisy in its dirt.
I've bandaged the Toyota.
I've dished out food for the beasts underground.

What, if anything, have I forgotten?
My heavens, my emergency,
my screams 'round the corner...?

Pay no attention to the freckles on my nose.

When I repair the flooded sink, the ceiling caves in.
I fill out my jeans with a denim colored pen.
I almost always know my way home.

But hey, what the fuck, I'm a star and always will be.

I do what I can for the accident victim.
I give him a biscuit, a sailboat, a key...

Some things get noticed right away, and some never at all.

One punchline upon another, then another and another...

The end drags on for a very long time.

ALL THE BEST REASONS I'M NOWHERE

I don't know whether I'm talking
or if I'm nineteen. I do know I need a haircut.
And the world opens its lips and spits plastic

army men straight-up like scotch in the movies
or a fountain of youthful exuberance, angels
and gargoyles pissing together. Everything

muddy: the curtain and the cowboy, the song
that he sings. In the background, a recording
of a man saying "shit" and "shirt" plays

loopy forever, while in the forecast
more snow and more snow, exceedingly.
I'm not sure of the wording exactly, but it's

yesterday again when I was up to my eyeballs
in sadness, which makes them red and tired and high
looking east, like dull berries in the light, like

two chicken hawks in the darkness. Even
this morning I'd already made a million mistakes.
I thought creativity counted more than a funeral.

I called you my snow shoe, etc. I said
I love you with my dearly in the headlights
and nothing mattered more. I was stupid

and I was stupid, but now I've stopped.

IN THE SAD LITTLE BEEP BEEP

Sometimes fluttering is all that's required.
Or the air, even blotted with lilacs, feels
like car horns blaring in the afterglow
of noon. So as a joke you sit down
with a clean sheet of paper and write
your own obituary, then post it around town,
where your old teachers will see it.
Included with the text is a shot of you grinning
and the headline: "X Never Made Eagle Scout,
But Was Devoted to Surrealism."
Everyone who reads it has a laugh about it, too.
It's the kind of thing they've come to expect
from you at the bottom of the planet,
spinning wolves out of wool, and sharks
out of pool. It makes you invincible and
promising, but also unnerving one night
when you don't come back from the grocery
or wake up, not even when they shake you.
Oscillation continues as the milk you bought
expires, or your memory goes out for strawberry
ice cream. And except for the three or four people
who really love you, you fade without thought
in a short-circuit of pigeons, landing and taking off
and molting. "X is survived by a traveling
circus. His engine remains
in its orbit."

IN DEFIANCE OF GRAVITY I CONNECTED THE DOTS

and there was some question,
at least in the minds
of all the things that fly,
whether I was any good
or just messing around.

Thus, I frowned
when the ceiling started
leaking its fluid
in judgment— too early
by my lights— soaking
my best efforts
at connecting the wings
of a moth to those
of a starling, and the wings
of a starling to those
of a gargoyle, and the wings
of a gargoyle to those
of da Vinci, and the wings
of da Vinci to those
of the Wright Bros., and the wings
of the Wright Bros. to those of an angel,
or devil, or piglet, etc....

when it flies, etc....

in the lead-dark, etc....

In the wings
there was obviously
some question

LITTLE GIVING NOISES

My body, I'm certain, is full of purple light.
This coffee is really coffee. My wrists
are screwed on and they aren't coming off...
Damn. Who am I kidding? I'm nobody
wise. The acres and acres of kale
go to waste. The black birds feast
on the hull of a love boat.
What's left for me to do
other than mambo?
Other than Christ in a spicy brown sauce?
Nowadays everybody knows:
you've seen one drop of blood
you've seen an ocean.
Clearly, I'm ashamed of my past in the theater,
my synthesizer performances,
my gangsta rap life.
My darling, what's frozen
stays frozen even in the heat
of the overblown nightmare.
But I swear to you,
it's all I have to offer.

HALF-EMPTY

In my stomach, green beans. In my mind,
green spaces. I bend at the waist and retrace
the inflatable lifeboat before my eyes. A sour
glass of milk. The black tips of gone matches.

Yesterday I washed a load of lights and darks
together. Now everyone's confused in the pinks.
Everyone, that is, except my mother, who thinks
I have a beautiful xylophone, no matter its color,

She loves me, and because of it, I can afford to spend
another night with my head inside a rabbit— Yippee!
Returning in the morning to my upright position, I see
crows swooping down on the clown's private happenings.

What luck! to be alive and engaged. So many different
duck calls, so many different peripheries, all neck and neck
for the same dizzy attention. The dead bird dog.
The goddess in a wetsuit. The dude with the glue

making everybody high. I spit up my lunch and the world
remains with me. My head in the lake
between drinking and sleeping. My love
between dawning and empty.

THIS IS CALLED PURE GREEN

This is called pure green:
this leaf
this schema
this sad little airplane
taking its wings too seriously
and thinking itself
a full-fledged flying thing.
This way irregular.
This way inexplicable.
Everything thick and grassy
and expressly defiant.
Ah well, says the janitor.
Touché, says the torch.
The chiropractor cracks his knuckles,
and his knuckles expect the worst—
when from out of nowhere
the parakeet chirps like a lion:
O emerald, forgive me,
the sky.

CALM POEM

Of all the calm poems I've written
this calm poem

is definitely my favorite.
It came at the end of a calamitous day—

I couldn't remember what to say
during a lecture.

I cried while reading
a philosophical preface.

When I looked in the mirror
I saw pieces of a blue jay

and the world turned
my stomach

in the gathering dust.
Forget it, said the poem.

Now you're safe at home.
Many people love you.

No need to create a scene.
No need to punctuate

the roar of the page.
Go to sleep and dream

you're a giant paper snowflake.
There is nothing to be afraid of.

MY HISTORY IN THE SHOWER

First I was a drop in the slow brain
of a cloud, and my father called me Molasses.
Heavier and heavier and colder and colder
I became, so my mother made me
a coat out of dread. I sailed

through school, reinventing the idiot,
and wrote what I could on the clean plastic walls.
Only later did I realize I had no choice in the matter.

The black walnut trees in my neighbor's yard stank.
I ate some perfumed soaps from a dish in the foyer,
only to discover I'd been whirling for hours.

The rain beat down until, finally relaxed,
I turned to the faucet and twisted the knob.
When I emerged from the drain, a man stopped
to crush me, offered his hair like a beautiful towel.

RETIREMENT PLAN

Suddenly it was raining again.
Time to give the old guy the ax.
He had been trying for years to assemble
a swan from a bunch of broken coat hangers,
but always the rain intervened. Or called-in
to check out the haze over his work station,
the volunteer fire fighters doused him
with the hose. We all knew his muse
must've rusted years ago, sticking him
in the muck between the stomach
and intestines. He never even made it over
to the box of feathers. Now the only question
was how to decorate the ax, how to make it
a party instead of a bloodstain. The usual
ways were either too sharp or too blunt, and
the old guy was fragile. Did he have any family?
None of us knew, but on mail day
he sat cross-legged under an umbrella
cursing the guts of his swan-in-progress
while the rest of us gorged ourselves
on pictures from home, trying to read
the captions before the ink ran.
What if we cranked up the ax so hard
that he didn't even recognize it as the ax?
What if he thought it was an extended fishing
trip or a birthday cake of coat hangers,
the very ones he'd been using
all these years. Maybe he'd think
we'd been saving them to surprise him.
He might even expect an award
for a job well done. But then a note
drifted downstairs to make the ax look like an ax.
So after work a bunch of us took him
to see a film about another old guy
who was trying to make a real boy
out of some pieces of kindling.
And he succeeded, sort of.
But then the wooden boy ran away
and fell in with some damaging characters
who turned him into a donkey. So the old guy
in the movie built a raft and went searching

for the wooden boy out on the ocean,
but he didn't get far before
he was swallowed by a whale.
At that point our old guy must've
gotten the idea, because he left his seat
and walked up the aisle. By the time he got
to the lobby he had his stone out and some oil.
And when he got back to the office
he sharpened the ax so keenly
that it was a single sheet of paper
with a place for his signature. Then
he opened his mouth and coughed up
several feathers. It was an expert
severance. He never knew what hit him.

WHERE IS YOUR HEAD IN THE GREATNESS, THE SCHEME?

Never mind looking for it, it's looking for you.
It has the eyes, you have the pipe organ.
It's in the trees with the owls.
It's talking politics and bubbles.
It's describing the sounds of the tuba as lovely
and declaiming your name to the heavens of the world
in a mustard-like, luminescent fog. I swear to god. What's god?

Never mind looking for Him, He's looking for you.
He has spotlights trained on the hills where you hide, screams
your perfect name into the caves and markets and strip malls
of history. Don't answer. Instead, kick up your heels and sing
to the crickets. The stars are a fortune we've yet to achieve.
Remember nothing you've been told. You are not a sad fence post
          waiting.
You are an astronaut with a wallpaper throat. See it?

Never hesitate to look where no one else has looked,
where kings with bombs cower under night-sheets sweating.
You are an electric eel. You are slippery and lithe. You have
          dynamite
in your nervous system. Beware of falling rocks. Fuck the
          falling rocks.
They make a great meal. Gravity is substance, and substance is
          the REAL.
Truth is what they feed you when they wanna make you false.
Beauty is the back of an elephant, a cemetery of sublimity,
          melting ice cream.

Never mind what flavor. The point is that the stream
of consciousness will save you, if always you traverse it
with an ever-ready spoon. Pay attention to the shadows
that are cast by the moon and the pangs in your veins,
so hysterically with joy. Once there was a boy who was eaten by a
          tiger,
which turned out to be a kind of a cobra, which turned out to be
a great white shark, a submarine, a warplane, an
          intercontinental ballistic...

Well, you can see how this works: one thing overtakes the next,
accumulating, leaping, pointing forward and back, always to
        reinvent
the facts, always to escape the limits, or to limit, by strictures, the
        infinities
of steam. Last night in my dream I looked into the sun, and for
        the very first time
I could see your face in the dark. Half-eaten breakfasts, lost
        seamen on lookout;
wind powered towers, soft-swaying like flags. Roosters with fangs.
Rechargeable oranges. Vociferous, unruly, bewitchments of dust.

I wasn't scared, and I wasn't. You were there too, and you weren't.
You had moved on to the next wishing well, I wish you well, I
        wish you wish you.
Never forget that I love you. Never put a wedge in your heart.
There is so much we don't believe and must, and so find at long
        last in the wintery mirror.

Never doubt for a second the grand catastrophe of self. Never
doubt the imaginative life, its twisted potential, its mountainous
        spirit going up/coming down in a flash
of death ashes. When things are most lost, your powers will find
        you.
Take notes. You'll thank yourself later.

I, BEING BORN OF SKIN AND UNDRESSED

I, being born of skin and undressed, expand
toward the end of a long table
where someone cracks an egg
on the side of a mixing bowl. There and then
I begin to breathe, and nearly immediately
someone reminds me of my interview at nine.
I tie on a tie and scarf down some toast.

At the interview the man's a real guy, stares
into me hard and sees the indifferent pigeons.
It's not so hot in there, he says, let me give you
some friendly advice. The way to impress
is to wear everything down to a nub,
to blackout in the tub, and then poof:
Watch me pull a rabbit out of my colon.

After that, real life begins. And soon I hear myself
saying plainly, If I can convince you
to fall apart on me, I can also convince you
to fall in love with me. It's all about
cloudbursts and yielding to the intrepid goslings.
It's all about the proper light, but more about
the proper darkness. It seems

I have an answer for everything.

HOW TO THINK LOGICALLY

If X is a proposition, then X is either True or False.
In more liberal systems X might also be classified
as indeterminate, but most leading logicians shy away
from this as it's less rigorous, and therefore,
allows for too many accidents on the job, which
has been shown to disrupt both Beauty and Truth.
That is, Perfection itself. Think trees and forests
and man-made service islands. The loss of limbs,
the use of thumbs, the best and the brightest.
For instance, "Kennedy was assassinated by Lee Harvey
Oswald," is True and Beautiful as a proposition
just in case and provided that one is speaking
of John F. Kennedy and not his brother Robert, who
at the time of John F's assassination was the Attorney
General of the United States, and furthermore provided
and just in case that Oswald worked alone and was not,
as he claimed, a patsy. Think baker man and shoeshine
boy and rub-a-dub-dubious. Always state clearly what each
important term means. White-collar, rabbits, and monkeys.
Do not forget to add the proviso that some very anxious
characters do not fit into any of these categories, and yet,
however sad or anxious they may be, are still possibly
presidential material. Logic compacts and simplifies
the exceedingly challenging and incalculable nature
of existence. Logic demonstrates the way things
should be, so that human beings might follow its example.
Think tire iron, congressperson, knock-knock joke.
Think sniveling, croaking, access denied. Scientists
are now agreed, there is no such substance as heat.
Heat is a quality. To abstract a quality is to remove it
from its associations and to consider it separately.
Lions and tigers and bears. Oh my and oh no and oh yes.
Logic tells us that a bundle of sticks cannot be easily
broken just because each one taken separately can be
easily broken. Think Adam and Eve and Steve. Logic
is completely apolitical and amoral, even when dis-
cussing fascism and the descent of man. Think
D. Alighieri and Orpheus and moles. For example,
the phrase "descent of man" has caused some
confusion among persons unfamiliar with how
scientists mean to use it. That is, it is sometimes felt

that the human race is considered by scientists
to be at a lower level than the amoeba or the ape.
This line of thinking is not perfect; in it there is a mistake.
What one comes to understand is that much is ambiguous,
and what logic seeks is clarification. Butter and glass
and ink. Some artists believe that logic is of little use
in their work, but what is art if not an emanation
of the spirit which attempts to achieve Truth and Beauty?
And as we've seen already, Truth is Beauty, and Beauty is
Truth, but Beauty is also Perfection, and Perfection is the back
of a cave. Think Rodin's "Thinker," Da Vinci's "Mona
Lisa," and Gaudier-Brzeska's "Hieratic Head of Ezra
Pound." One feels in logic like one is getting on
with one's nose, like one's waistcoat is being unfastened
for the first time, and the air is refreshing. Soldiers
can be classified and re-classified and AWOL. Consider
men who fire muskets, men who support the revolution
and conscientious objectors. Always, one stands
against the wall and waits for death in the face.
Or sometimes the names of beaches and parks and
the shadow hiding under the wallpaper.
In a textbook on geometry a point is always
necessarily represented by a dot, even though a point,
being an abstraction, has no actual dimensions. Think
people with dogs and skated spirals and STDs.
In logic perseverance is the same as deliverance
from evil. One considers everything in concert
and swoons fastidiously, but without motion.
Always, if this, then that,
or nothing.

DIRIGIBLE. DOG BREATH. TIMBUKTU.

If you are a lava lamp, then I am a broken
heating element, then the freezer stays cooler
and we are preserved as smoldering finches
and blood oranges.

If a balloon in your mouth feels like hooray
followed by a cotton seed, followed by a tumor,
then the sanitarium is unnecessary
as you are deeply exploding.

If the report comes back, No intelligent life,
then no breath, no maraschino cherries, no
antennae, no win.

Here, I can only think: clog, puff of smoke,
abstract blob of burned plastic bags.

Everything in this house of ants and lizards,
from the firecrackers down to the fat lady smoking
cigarettes on the buckling ice rink,
is conditional.

If I'm the one who never forgets, then you two
never remember.

REMODELING

Tarpaper hat. Home of the burning ostrich.
Teeth of the man screwed into despair.
I'm told at breakfast that I should be making people cry

and later that I should avoid looking at young women
on their way to the dentist or the exploded library.
Still later I'm told that someday I'm going to ask
my audience to forgive me for writing a lecture

called "Breaking the Dog and/or Kissing the Scarecrow."
Naturally I breathe this like pitch in my lungs,
and with a flurry of bell peppers I burst into tears

because suddenly I can't deny anything. And what's worse,
I can't deny everything. The floors are made, and I walk
on them as if they never happened. The ceiling fan wishes.
The roof of nails whines. If it fails, I'll be crushed

in a mess of plastic flowers. Make no mistake,
the sky is falling. A talking hen told me. We're all
in this together, she said, but we don't often think

it's significant. So after the big game called breakfast,
I withdraw to the park and brood over the art market.
What's this picture worth? And why can't I find it
in a book? What can I get for Radio Pain? How 'bout

Belly Ache Per Usual? And that sculpture, A Number Called
Devil? What ever became of Blue Death and Pieces?
Why does the mess that I started with glow?

Hey you, reader, I'm no speaker.
I'm the guy writing this, the guy who just wrote this,
a guy who has been M*** H***, thirty years old.
It's July 18, 2004. He fights with my wife, but I'm okay.

GIANT TRAUMATISM

— after Guillaume Apollinaire

The carpet fades from red to green
From bottom to top in the invisible metropolis
Dignitaries whistle their pitiless speeches
Surgery's massive reductions
Paul sweeping leaves from his side of the driveway
There is a message to be written on the changing of the season
From carriage to pumpkin, Cinderella had her fun
Small contaminant pieces
But what's to be done in the aftermath's gloaming
If X is a chimp under the influence of silence
Today's tarts are still in the freezer and must be thawed
Feel sorry if you want to, but the sun is shining
The sounds of garbage trucks
Jaws of life
You will pull the pitted incisor
The doorknob, the hinges, let velocity be your guide
And now take a look through the peephole in the floor
An indecency of apes goes about its merry business
A lamp lights the way to the end of the bar
Lawn mower, earthworm, mockingbird stew
Down in the face, the man catches on: this life is fun and no fun
Ha ha! says the wife when she lays out the doormat
Truly, an old woman lived in a shoe
Who is the meaning of this
What is the patter in the young man's chest
We will make cupcakes
We will surprise our guests with gusto and flashing, miniature
          cameras and pelvic vibrations
We shall try in vain to arouse torte feasance
Forget the turn signal
A tern is a bird
We no longer need climax; now we just shimmer
Everyone feel something delightful
Our breath out before us rings with the visible force of revolution
Give us the clamp and the suction to make it
Our culture is thriving to the honking of horns
O thick in the snow
O barely alive
The red carpet pulled up for a green one tomorrow

Chicago New York San Antonio Berkeley Tucson Pittsburgh
    Price Hill and Paris
The jaws bite down on all of us spinning
Lovely last looks on our faces

PET CRICKET

Paula's note says: you have to make it
worse before you make it, so I buckle down
and worry the evidence into pieces of a cricket.

And now, even though the leg still kicks a little
when the lights come on, it just hasn't been
the same since it separated from the thorax.

Thus, while one doctor makes an incorrect diagnosis,
and another squirrels away syringes for the party,
I wait with a glass of Pernod, clicking my heels.

If the guest list contains a hundred names
and all of them arrive at eight hundred hours,
then how fast will the bartenders have to move

in order to serve everyone before Paula says
something flashy and shoots me into a coma
of flowers? For example, *The grammar of gardening*

collapses. Is it true we're in a struggle with language?
Because that's not at all what I expected. I was hoping
for great white sharks or parking tickets, bad seats

at the symphony. Poor little guy. How 'bout some
euphony over here? He's fibrillating something awful,
flipping around in a circle. He's had it. Please,
somebody get him some dope for the pain.

NOW THAT I HAVE EATEN THE LORD MY GOD

My Manager's name is impossible to say,
His motives impossible to know.

He loves me, He loves me not,
which creates, in spite of my knowing better,
a vision of something two-headed,
inestimably perspicuous with teeth
made for tearing. Damned
as I am dearly saved, I owe somebody something big.

But where O where are You tonight?
Why did You leave me here all alone?

I want my want and need my need
and feel my feeling to the utmost.
My Manager, thou hast made it so.

And yet, Thine image is too big for my britches.
Thy charm, the nature of birds in the sky.
I wrestle oblivion. I sweep up
my messes. I find myself wishing
the end of the world.

ADDRESS TO THE RHINOCEROS

Welcome at last! odd-toed, fearsome land-version of the
    hippopotamus.
I think you're angelic, the way you almost rhyme with dust and
    serve us
as both runway and pit-stop for scores of those little black birds
who are the messengers of god. Reading about you I learned the
    word
keratinous (more later), and I learned that you are non-
    ruminant, which
means that you neither re-chew your food (even though you eat
    nothing
but fiber!), nor meditate with hands clasped in prayerful
    reverence, as
each second the ultra-violets beat down on your hardy, unkillable
    skin.
Those horns on your snout parry whatever with heat and
    charge—
flowers, the wind... On second thought, no, please do not charge.
I am not a rival male, nor am I a (lost) matador. I am
    unimaginable
(judging by the look on your face— lackadaisical, radiant, much
    muchness),
and I'm wondering at the tire of your neck, the wire of your tail,
    and also
that which comes from the Latin word *cornus* and the Greek
word *keras*, from where we get *keratin* (a sulfur-based fibrous
    protein),
the primary ingredient in all sorts of epidermal tissues: hair,
    skin, feathers,
and yes, you guessed it— horns. I'd like to see you trash
a lovely home on Cape Cod just because. I could help you escape
from the zoo. Do you ever go over anything in your mind
    repeatedly
the way I do? Sometimes I think I don't matter at all. Do you
ever think at all? Matter at all? Worry? I'd like to be one of
    those
little black birds on your head, or better just the message he
    carries:
a few words about slouching, a few mumbled commandments.
The universe is crushing. Rhinoceros, break it.

WHAT'S INSIDE A GIRAFFE?

Elevators going up.
The guts and black stuff of three in the morning.
An interminable list of romantic O's.
The sigh at the end of a night-long dream.
Unexpected, excellent, sausage!
Factory churning full-tilt over the wall.
Definitely Negative Capability.
Certainly the first limousine.
Echoes and re-echoes, Echoes and re-echoes, Echoes and re-
      echoes...
Narcissus.
Mommy, I'm thirsty.
Somebody give me a beer.
Evening caught in a parasol weeping.
Nerval out walking his lobster on a leash.
Rooftops.
Postmarks.
Two kids making-out in a bottomless pit.
All day, Saturday, piles of brown leaves.
An expert on bees on his deathbed buzzing.
The rockets, their red glaring error included.
What is is.
A pack of wild dogs.
The collected equations of Benjamin Péret.
Youssou N'Dour, Salif Keita, Oliver Mtukudzi, King Sunny Ade.
What a circus ought to be.
A song of sadness in an elephant box.
The ends of the earth.
Saliva for miles.
The exuberance missing in today's ice cream.
The hottest band in the world.
Cannoli filled with orange/bay leaf marzipan cheese, then dipped
      in chocolate and served on a plate of tropical fruit and
      sprinkled with powdered sugar.
The taste of raw oysters.
The shadow of Guillaume Apollinaire.
Conjunction junction, its function besides.
Cats in the hallway screaming their lives.
Information arranged in columns and sorted by zip code.
She loves me, she loves me not, endlessly.
Who you callin' whitey?

Trickle down economics.
The crabgrass amazed.
The canary in its office smacking into glass.
Things are looking up, are they not?
Welcome to gravity's impossible party.
Philosophical investigations.
How about a walnut the size of a brain?.
How about an accordion that never shuts up?
Nothing comes immediately to mind, and then it just sits there.
A big, fat liver.
Polyester stuffing and an air-powered squeak toy.
What used to be a tugboat is now a digested life preserver.
O clogged gutters will you ever come clean?
Distracted by exercise, charmed by fools, the windmills.
I blush to think of it.
Feed the dog. Take a shower. Eat breakfast.
Pop goes the weasel.
Bananas and toast and a sundae with nuts.
Babble.
Rubble.
Toil and trouble.
The unraveling of X, the poems hot 'n' heavy.
The afternoon flying a jet through your hair.
Absolutely everything, even dust.
Where "I" is most certainly somebody else, what have you in the
        way of identity politics?
Not Brian Vanaski.
Not a really colorful tattoo.
More procrastination than I know how to use effectively.
The hallowed halls of bureaucracy.
Spelling "estuary" correctly.
A cure for esophageal cancer.
The proper method for modeling a turtleneck.
The distance from here to your mother in spots.
From there to your father in shredded coconut.
Why pregnancy isn't an option.
If you stand on your toes you can just make out the mountains.
A brand new Uncle Wiggly.
Survey says...
Splendiferous evening on front porch swinging.
Swallows falling out of the very worst trees.
Toy box. Solar system. Fertilizer spreader.
Time for the 7th inning stretch.
Ball of string.
Vertical tight rope.

A distant cough.
Somebody's bread and butter.
The punctum.
Whereas it used to be required knowledge for getting into heaven,
        now it's only a suggestion.
Eucalyptus, Mentholyptus, Citrus.
That's a wrap.
Let's meet back here in five minutes.
I'm still in need of a cotton ball, an SOS pad, and a picture of a
        lawnmower from the SEARS catalogue, Winter, 1975.
Duck-duck-goose.
Rock-Paper-Scissors.
Who put the bop in the bop-sha-bop-sha-bop, who put the ram in
        the ram-a-lam-a-ding dong.
Also, who wrote the book of love.
Who died trying.
With the big, ugly voice of Ethel Merman.
They saved Hitler's cock.
Incredibly powerful gag reflex.
Poor Gepetto.
The end of tap dancing.
Abecedarian.
Smooth sailing.
Rapidly approaching, a cherry blossom!
Long goodbye.
African Queen.
Size does matter, doesn't it?
A new kind of not-maple syrup.
Door prizes ranging from 1-1000 dollars.
Where the inside ends and the outside begins— that is most
        definitely the mystery.
It is written in mud, it is written on the fly.
Wild Dobby Gibson, burgled by dusk.
Strawberry fields forever.
Breaking apart on the outskirts of space.
Anything by John Cage.
Anything involving the use of a hammer.
Anything by John Cage involving the use of a hammer.
Idi Amin.
Your family having dinner.
The contents of the giraffe's stomach— primarily leaves.

SONG, NOT FROM MY HEART

My bone-plate head, enormous.
My well-made head in the furnace.
My ferocious maneuver head.
My insistent, pneumatic and billowy head.
It houses the plans for my lemonade stand.
Someday, I'll write down what I meant, or instead...
My head on the workings of straw.

My dastardly head of the present.
My marmalade head over breakfast.
My staring-at-air fish head.
My tripped and hit the pavement head.
There's someone else in there, and he's breaking the glass.
If I could I'd forget him and sleep through his shred...
My head with its numerous saws.

My letter head speaking absurdist.
My spiral bound head of recurrence.
My chipped to bits revision head.
My parakeet fair-weather lollygag head.
I tried to remember the back of my hand.
I tried to remember, but started to bleed.
My head of electrified moth.

MORNING COLLAGE

Three red squares
and a burnt, French writer.
As an afterthought,
I crossed out the dog.

ONLY A TRANSMITTER

Now that I've stopped shouting and started listening
to the radio, I'm understanding more and more the ways

to unfold myself, both to the beginnings and ends of things,
things I can't be sure ever/even really happen. In spite of this,

I'm often hit with a brilliant flashlight. Often I'm thrown
into dizzy speculation: now we're nearing the noumena;

now the curtain is rising on a whole new era... Either way
I'm exhausted and feverishly congested, most of my waking life

spent walking in my dreams— a dog pissing gold-leaf, a daughter
burning out the sun. Today I blew my nose in a retail store

and thus trumpeted the general irritation everyone was feeling
but couldn't bring themselves to acknowledge in public.

When I tell you I'm only a transmitter, when I sound off
my beeping life as both shepherd and keeper of the jar

of my mind, all I'm really saying is I don't have anyone
to talk to, and when I do, I confuse them with chatter

and noise. Isn't there a manual I can read for my life,
a drippy faucet I can fix or an appetizer to invent?

I communicate best when digesting an avalanche.
I pay as I go, and (I go) incessantly, rolls of quarters

like peaches off a tree, like astronauts blipping out
in a mudslide. What a Messy Bessy I've become

in my spare time. I know nothing at all of the fortune
I crave, how to tell the truth plainly from finish to start.

My style is no style. My form a pigsty.
Just look how far I haven't come in the dark.

STRANGER IN FAMILIAR TERRITORY

Beautiful, luminous, man with potatoes,
forgive me, I'm not used to waking up in the dirt.
I'm not used to my head on the end of a stick,
nor hanging for my life on the edge of the world.
If this is confusion, it pains me. If gold leaf,
then I know not how to spin it into straw. At once
I am a body and nobody. Clearly, I'm the mud
in my mouth. When I sign my name I recognize it
completely, a real definition of what I ought to be:
free in the face to erupt like a toad, to come
clean in the carwash of heaven. Your face is all I have
to remind me of home, to anchor my body
in the various earth, some red and some yellow
and some with decorative patterns, floating
like smoke in the sky in the night. When I
was a factory, unstable and predatory, I let
the light bulb have its way in the dark, I cried
in the back of the schoolgirl's Mercedes. But now
I spread myself on toast and have breakfast.
I make for the alley and take off my coat.
I take off my pants, my underwear and socks.
And the more I give up, the more invisible
you become, until finally I can't see a thing.

FACE FIRST INTO THE DARKNESS

Say Here when your name is called
even if it's not the right name. Especially
if it's gravity. Especially I melt.
I can already tell
the thing this needs
is a lot more powerful feeling, a lot more
sincerity, a lot more
self-doubt. So if you'll excuse me a moment,
I think I may have something in the basement that'll do the trick.
In the meantime, kick back and enjoy this wave
of squealing feedback.
Shout it out loud. Brain of saltines.
Rest in peace or in pieces. Lost and found later
in a room with my throat,
picking up garbage, ascending some stairs.
And now that we're in paradise, how are your ears?
Is the ringing too much, too little, too bright?
Always the fight goes sour in the moonlight,
The flutter, the empty, the blood-soaked cocoon.
Boom boom boom, says another dead star.
If you were actually here with me and gesturing come hither,
I'd mimic every movement and take the whole thing too far.
Another execution, another sexy tulip.
Bursting one's bubble is a serious offense.
Miracle cures are the only ones left.
Ice cream parlor, ocean at midnight,
the big fluorescent light store where nobody's home.
I'm throwing my voice to imitate love.
Nobody hears when you fall.

CONFETTI

Broken space, then singing machine.
I heard the music from four blocks away.
Why didn't I know where any of it was going?

The stick figure said, Goner.
A window closed, but only a crack.
Down the street

the beast wouldn't take my devil,
the one who was 3'3" exactly,
the one who came to me, and who I nailed

together waiting for you to say the things
I've squirmed to hear: my Indefensible, my As You Are.
Where oh where is my Absentee? Linoleum mistake.

Half-exploded dish. I'm defending you— myself,
somebody... Eyelids bent. Corsage on blocks.
If you want we can do it tonight.

HEREIN

lies the beginning and end.
Herein a patrol car.
Herein a grain silo.
Herein the heart of my love at the dance
is spinning and spinning and spinning.
If she is looking in my direction
I have nothing to fear
even herein beset by spirits,
the spirits of tigers, the spirits of bears, the spirits
of fathers passed out in the snow.
Herein language takes a nosedive into rocks.
Herein I've pissed off my mother by phone.
When the death-god squirms herein,
the atom bomb stirs herein.
Some days herein, the wires
go numb, heads of state waving from the door
of a plane. Some days the head on its own
rolls away; some days the mouth causes terrible trouble.
Herein a tugboat is crying for more.
The garbage man and jellyfish, herein. Swimming
down the drain, herein. Herein, herein...
Herein the sad, waking dream becomes a mantra.
Herein blaze and the sickening future,
the song of the watchman telling his time,
the watchmaker staring out the window at a clock.
How can I return to my love herein?
And what will I find when I find her?
The transistor radio like a puppy all night.
The elephant forgetting where he started to fall.
In the wake of exhaustion, the body feels heavy.
Then a moment of vacuum-like silence.

IN HUMAN RESONANCE

Lounging in my blue suit,
it's almost noon, and I am
preparing to damage my art books.
Toulouse Lautrec attacked by sharks.
Paul Klee gone missing in a duel with frogs.

Mike is over fixing the furnace,
and the house smells like burning dust.
To speak in code is to relax. Saturday
again. Hailstorm works. Quotes Coleridge best,
who lovest best. Thank you sad astronaut.

Thank you in advance professor Y, my hair
growing longer by the minute. In the meantime
I answer an unglued subscriber: Dear Guy,
Sorry to inform you we have folded our napkins
and put away the silver. The PO Box collapsed.
Do not hold your breath. We are deep
incommunicado. Yours disconnected,
Uncle Dispersion

Probably the tone of it will end up mistaken.
Lunch in the furnace: hot peppers and decaf.
Mike says the former is bad for my stomach.
The latter is hard on your liver. The first

is a paraphrase, the second a quote. Note
the falling off, the loss of intensity.
O monster, don't flutter, come back.

SPRING CLOTTING

I'm not sure what it is, but there's more blood today.
Maybe we should find a mop. Then again, it is in a frame
— let's discuss aesthetics! The blurb says, *Any suggestions
can be registered with the ad hoc propter hoc...*

But enough about me. Shall I call mall security
or will we leave peaceably? I'm no flower salesman,
I'm a suckling-after-spring, and I can't see a thing
for all this hemorrhaging. That is the proper term, is it not?

I'm never precise enough, which is only one of my flaws,
but suddenly it's anathema to groping you in the car,
the fuzzy dice between us, all possibles swinging.
Remember how the butcher wrapped the meat in white paper,

how we walked around backwards for hours digesting?
You were ground beef and I was the army. The flies
were immense and the noise unbearable— the atonal singing,
the gurgling zoo. It wasn't your voice I objected to.

In fact I have always loved the way you read the classics,
your mouth like nothing on the nightly news. Still, I'm just
one mask soaked through with preserves, so take these bursts
for what they point to. The moon frequently plussed by udders.

Grandma out shopping comes back as wolves. I've been
pulling her teeth for a fortnight now. She screams my name,
and I slam the door hard. Somebody has to make the universe
safe. Each night falling asleep at the wheel, I think, one more

as hell's periscope, one more as the surgeon who lurks
in the bushes. But delicate operations keep dragging me
to this wall. My luck is a burst appendix, and this, my only
instruction manual. Press this gauze compress against me.

KNOCK KNOCK KNOCK

Saddest think-tank on the block,
Who's home? What's there?

— A rock in my shoe.
— There's a rock in your shoe?

— Yes. And the new cashier has a pity
on her face. — A pity on her face?

Indeed. Who's there? — The woozy raccoon
who would like to thank his mother

for bringing him into the whorl,
for twirling him into the dance. Meanwhile,

the cashier at home goes blind
with agony. — Knocked-up Antigone?

— No, seriously. Stayed up all night re:
arranging the locks. Hydroelectric, said the fox.

The dams won't give, not a lick. — Not even in this?
— Nope. Not knot gnosis. When one gets lost,

one should get lobster. — A plastic lobster?
— A view of the world. — A view of the world,

who? — I said one should get loster. One should get her
jam on. One should knock it 'til it bleeds.

REVELATED

When the house started blowing forward
on its hinges, I was sitting in the backyard
worrying about how my body might bloom

out of season, thus paralyzing myself
for the third time in as many minutes.
But the house, gray-blue and disenchanted

with its anti-depressants and goose-down pillows,
pitched me the news flash: Man, you will be
crushed again and crushed good,

which released me in a weird, not unpleasant,
sort of way. And that's when I invited the black ants
to take over the life masks on the mantel.

My brain reddened with dust, and I remembered
the feeling of living. To the cat food left out, I said,
The swarm cometh, prepare to be blackened.

The gutter banged a rhythm on the side of my skull.
All the while, hard pressed to understand the wind,
so dramatically pleasing and destructive at the same time,

the house expanded first around me, then
through me, a montage of serums, flypaper and bricks.
The ant colonists, too, groaned and grew, drowned

the little radio in automatic waves. Everything I knew
was razored to ash, so I turned my attention
to the panoply of heaven. What else could I do? The stars

winked on a billion nights. The daughter returned
to show off her thighs. Narcotic ever after, I was kept
in a blind spot, pinned to the sky by a house.

HAILSTORM

An agony afoot, I burst into peacocks,
Reverdy all afternoon. Loss for loss,

nothing is easy. In one poem a horse
jumps flatly over a hedge of sparks,

the horseman blue. And a bone or a flower
is clouded with silence, everything engulfed

in the peripheral. Somehow this produces in me
pain, an unquenchable line of amputees.

As far as the eye can see them
they are walking into the sea. Yesterday,

Saturday, totally scarecrow, empty as a January
ice cream parlor, I wondered how to say

complicated in a less complicated way, how
to say abstraction and mean something actual.

And I thought of calling you, or writing a letter,
but I've been masquerading lately as a barrel

of monkeys presented all at once from every
angle. Life is a beautiful hailstorm, which is kind

of forlorn and scenic all at the same time. Or put
another way I am an out-of-work oboe player.

I wonder if anyone other than you
can detect my sincerity? And I wonder, too,

when I leave a party, is everyone relieved
that the snowflake was only a terrible dream,

do they return to their drinking and summer?
I knew I would miss you, and I do.

AT THE MOMENT I AM UNWILLING

but it isn't so much the line of inquiry as the lack of it
that bothers me. My abdomen, and all else, seems
relatively sewn up. Once in a while a candy apple

oozes over the hood of my car, but otherwise
nothing spectacular happens. For instance
I hold my breath between two fingers and wilt
into an amplified lack of particular circumstances.

No one does his banking. No one walks her dog.
I wish and the wishes appear to me as shoddy brown
leaves on the workroom floor. Sorry, by the way,
to the mole I broke yesterday in the yard. Another

living thing put out of its mystery. The question then
becomes, Why resist wishful thinking at all
when life is a cabaret of propellers and spleens?
As one beam of light fires onto the screen,

another lonely bulb burns out in the kitchen.
My wife feels sorry for the distress this causes me.
A tarpaper mousetrap prevails in my head.
Years ago I set sail for a new kind of heaven,

one where creation is beginning again. Now someone buries
my parakeet feet. I can't find the world.

THE WILDER SHORES OF LOVE

Tell me, do you really think we're defined
by what we choose to ignore? Because by my lights
that's the whole world, which is somehow too big and intangible
to be scary. And yet, I'm afraid of everything and say it
with confidence.

I hear myself saying also, and with even more emphasis,
that we're defined by the people who break us open
and scrape out our hearts with a long-handled spoon.

And yet, I can't remember the last time I felt
certain of anything, not even a carrot, not even
a piece of wool. A dry-dive taken in a January pool.
And always to get back to the sound of waves.
And always for a sharper image.
I'd cut out my ear bones if I thought it would help,
the hammer and the drum and the little bleeding bird.
Let's skip all the stuff about chemical agents,
the soulmate transformed into somebody's grave.
In the final moment we're frying eggs
on a frozen sidewalk. How could things be any clearer?

You in your purple dress. Me
sweating in the snow.

WILDEBEEST

It's obvious: wild beast, suggesting an uncontainable
nature: kicking the lamp light, upsetting the roses.
But in fact the wildebeest is a gnu, and therefore
a member of the antelope family, which although wild
lacks something of the beast part. Perhaps a clue
to the wildebeest's nature is to be found in the French,
Gnou Bleu, or blue gnu, which sounds so much like
Who knew? that one can't help but see
the wildebeest for the paradoxical creature that it is:
bewildered with a passion for the sea. Furthermore,
the blue suggests a sort of melancholy
which does indeed seem to follow the wildebeest,
along with a strong, crumbly accent that hangs about
in the general vicinity wherever wildebeests are present.
But do not be fooled. The word *gnu* re-arranged
is *gun.* And like guns, wildebeests have been known
to go off without warning (on each other and strangers),
using their heads to do serious damage in the process.
For years they've resisted the closing of the so-called
"gnu-show loophole," which allows them
to go berserk without the usual background effects.
Any person unfortunate enough to encounter a loose wildebeest
should report it immediately to local emergency management
officials. In appearance, the wildebeest resembles a cross
between a goat and a cow, with the legs of a deer and the face
of a boarded-up saloon. Some are brindled, but others
are flat-gray or onyx with wavy, white tails
creating the illusion of an animal in surrender.

THROATINGS

Sometime after midnight, Christian went home
and Melanie went to bed. But I stayed up listening
to the makeshift wind chimes that hang near

the back door— bits of a broken ceramic vase,
drilled through and tied with craft wire, then hung

from a metal rod, which somebody (not us) mounted
to the brick of the house, brick that many landlords ago
was painted sky-blue and now peels. In the wind

the chimes sound like voices, but voices
in a language I can never make out, like the half-

electric throatings I'm listening to now, like
the green and blue bowls I'm washing,
banging together with three forks and a large pot,

the well-used skillet with the super-dented rim;
I don't feel so young anymore. But it's all good

because I don't feel particularly impossible either.
I'm somewhere between punk rock and a funeral.
And yet I have both in my head and chest at all times,

everything so centrally blown out of proportion
that living simmers completely in the present,

where now is always another truck of books
or playing "Serve the Servants" and singing along
until I'm light-headed, thinking of my wife, my friends,

myself, all of us existing in a singular quiet
saturation of incredulity and sadness.

When the rain begins to fall, it splatters in
on the white window sills.

I finish the dishes and talk to myself.
The end isn't anywhere

TO THE PEOPLE WHO KNOW BETTER, LET ME SAY IN MY DEFENSE

I am of the mind
and then
sadly insufficient.

I am of the gut
and then glued
to a wall.

Or plastered
like news
to the bottom
of a birdcage,

I am the shadows
of things in space.

There are
no more birds.

The sky
is a big holy
mouth.

I am

of the testicles.
As a result
something
swims for its life
and expires.
But before that
it cries
in a garden
under water.

Everywhere
there are other
crying, swimming
things
and beautiful

flowers,
simmering.

There are
no more birds.

My bone
has some meat
on it. The dog
dotes. The cat
takes a bath.
She is what
I call Disinterested.

Disinterested,
come and get it.
Disinterested,
have a treat.
The ball-
of-yarn cliché
is Disinterested's
favorite.

I am my own
dish rag.

I am my own
bent spoon.

I am of the nostrils
and as a result
often
get sucked
into mazes.
Monsters
attack me,
and always
it amazes,
but always
I prevail,
for I am of
Disinterested's
ball-of-confusion cliché,
and I do creep.

For I can swim
against
the wood
grain, for I
can cry
myself
to exhaustion
under the stars,
and, fact
of all facts,
for I have done
nothing wrong.

I am

of the bed sheets,
the rabbit hole,
the sewer hole,
the Epsom Salts.

My bones
become the dogs
of disinterest.

Two blue
feathers
are all
I have left.

When I hurt
it's bad,
but when
my love hurts
it's worse, almost
a hearse-hurt.
I take
a new breath
and give it
to her.

She would
do the same
for me.
In this way,

we rely
on one another.

But in other ways,
we are
of the difference.

Sometimes
between us
there is friction
in the kitchen,
and thus
we roast
a sea bass
or thus
we cook
a stew.

Sometimes
we make our
friction
into what
she said
and what
I didn't say.

Always
there are words:

I am of the heart,
the kind with wings,
the inefficient
splattered kind,
the heart
with its agenda
bringing
prescriptions
to the world,
the heart
with its notions
about new kinds
of birds
and yanking
those wisdom teeth out.

I am of the toy chest,
treasure chest,
amplifier,
ear drum...

Listen.

Okay.

I have a key
to a door
in the Bahamas.
I have a makeshift
water lily
in a glass.
You can
look at my chassis
and I will look
at your undercarriage,
and everything
will be alright.

Everybody needs
adjustment sometimes:

Twist these hairs
for lightning.
Tighten this
hinge
for love.

In the end—
is it the end?

I am of the sincerest
apologies
and best wishes

always,

also pronouncements
unbelievable and long

and disagreeables
living in the same
parking lot,

like a litter
of squirmy
new kittens
and a hearse.

Disinterested
isn't a fan
of my kittens,
but I will defend
them at all costs.
For I am of the mind

that belief
is better
than the heavy
truth of cream—

and then I change
my mind.

I am of a new sort,
one that hasn't even
been invented yet,
one that will cover
the dance floor
and one
that will sing
in the surf.

I am pleading

with the surf
to respond in kind.

I am pleading

with the dance floor
to commit.

In the end—
is it the end?

No, it's only
the sentimental
fadeout,

and I am very new
to this sort
of demonstration—
how to dust a landscape,
how to build a q-tip.
how to be

of the world outside
and also of this one
I found in a drawer.

You who know better,
know more,

how to do this
correctly,
and how to undo it
perfectly,
how to go
about it
in history,
what measures to take.

Write me
about anything.

The sky is full of words.

I am awaiting
your reply.

ACKNOWLEDGMENTS

Many thanks to the editors of the journals in which these poems first appeared: *Alice Blue* ("Completely by Accident"); *The Butcher Shop* ("The Weight of My Next Best Thing"); *The Canary* ("I Was Dumb with Pearls, I Was Dumb"); *Diagram* ("This Is Called Pure Green" and "What's Inside a Giraffe?"); *88* ("At the Moment I Am Unwilling," "Dirigible. Dog Breath. Timbuktu.," "Dada's Sawed-Off Half Brother," "In Human Resonance," and "In the Sad Little Beep Beep"); *The Greensboro Review* ("Spring Clotting"); *H_ NGM_ N* ("Calm Poem," "In Fifteen Minutes," "Letter to a Friend Who I'll Never See Again," and "Throatings"); *Incliner* ("Great White Shark"); *Konundrum Engine Literary Review* ("Elephant" and "To the People Who Know Better, Let Me Say in My Defense"); *Octopus* ("In the Gloaming"); *Painted Bride Quarterly* ("Giant Traumatism"); *Pip Lit* ("How I Know I'm Still Missing" and "Morning Collage"); *Ploughshares* ("Hailstorm" and "Inc."); *Puppy Flowers* ("Criss-Cross in Every Direction," "Retirement Plan," and "Self-Helper"); *River City* ("Breakable Swan," "Stranger in Familiar Territory," and "The Wilder Shores of Love"); *Salt Hill* ("Beautiful Burns"); *Slope* ("Address to the Rhinoceros," "Confetti," "Pet Cricket," "Song, Not from My Heart," and "Shag Carpet Gala"); *Spinning Jenny* ("I, Being Born of Skin and Undressed," "Only a Transmitter," and "Remodeling"); *Spork* ("How to Think Logically" and "Wildebeest"); *Spout* ("My History in the Shower" and "Revelated"); *Stirring* ("Apology Crisis"); *The Vocabula Review* ("Knock Knock Knock"); and *Words on Walls* ("All the Best Reasons I'm Nowhere," "As with Everything We Love," and "Little Giving Noises,")

"Knock Knock Knock" also appeared in the *The Vocabula Review's* print anthology *Vocabula Bound.*

"Twinge" was published by the Linda Schwartz Gallery in the catalogue for painter Kim Krause's *Greek Variations* in January, 2002.

Several of these poems also appeared in radically different form as collaged lyrics on the CD *B'Sides* by Travel, released by Starfish LE, 2005.

Many thanks to my friends and teachers for their encouragement, support and genius:

The Harts, The Holters, Mary Anne & Mike Cowgill, Christian Schmit, Darren Callahan, Liz Hildreth, Dave Rutschman, Frances Sjoberg, Paula Szuchman, Ethan Paquin, Thomas Heise, Darcie Dennigan, Meghan O'Rourke, Rachel Flynn, Sarah Manguso, Nate Pritts, Dobby Gibson, Grant Barber, Evan Commander, Brett Price, Sara Fraser, Jane Carver, Mike Vallera, Will Hutchinson, Scott Dennis, Zach Bowman

Patti White, Terri Ford, Pete Turchi, Ellen Bryant Voigt, Brooks Haxton, Stuart Dischell, Laura Kasischke, Heather McHugh, Tony Hoagland, and Dean Young

Eric Appleby, my brother.

This book is for Melanie, without whom I would sink.